**101 conversation starters** for families

**101 conversation starters** for families

# GARY CHAPMAN

## & RAMON PRESSON

Northfield Publishing
CHICAGO

ISBN: 978-0-8024-0839-6

We hope you enjoy this book from Northfield Publishing.
Our goal is to provide high-quality, thought-provoking books
and products that connect truth to your real needs and challenges.
For more information on other books and products written
and produced from a biblical perspective, go to
www.moodypublishers.com or write to:

Northfield Publishing
820 N. LaSalle Boulevard
Chicago, IL 60610

1 3 5 7 9 10 8 6 4 2

*Printed in the United States of America*

## Tips for Using 101 Conversation Starters for Families

One of the signs of a healthy family is open and meaningful communication. Good questions are the beginning. Here are some ways to use the questions:

• During dinner at home

• During a quiet moment in the evening

• Just before bedtime

• While in the car during a long drive

• On vacations

Parents, introduce the idea to your children and teens by describing this product as a game. Don't sell it as some serious communication project your family is going to work on. Note that the questions are designed to interest most school-age children and teenagers.

Therefore, every question encourages participation from every family member. Parents may want to secure agreement on a few ground rules:

- If you don't want to answer a question, you don't have to.

- If you can't think of an answer at the moment, your response will certainly be welcome at a later time.

- When someone is sharing an answer, everyone else will listen attentively without interrupting.

- All genuine responses will be respected and affirmed.

While the easiest way to proceed through the questions is to use them in the order they are presented, another possibility is to allow family members to take turns in selecting the questions. We recommend that you do only one or two questions at a time. And don't do them every day. Make your children ask for more, not less. These questions are like dessert—a small and satisfying portion creates the anticipation for more later. *101 Conversation Starters for Families* is great for single-parent and blended families as well.

Have fun with these questions a few times a week and enjoy the improved family communication.

Give each member of the family
an imaginary award for an
achievement or something
special they did recently.

conversation starters for families

Name one talent
you wish you had.

question
**2**
conversation starters for families

If you had to give up sight,
hearing, the ability to speak,
or the ability to walk,
which would you choose?

If you had a magic wand
and could change anything
in your life right now,
what would it be?

If you could be on any magazine cover, which one would you select?

If you could go on a vacation to another country, which one would you select?

What is one of your favorite stories that your parent(s) tell about you?

If we had to move from our home to another city, what would you miss the most about our home? Our neighborhood? Our city? Who would you miss the most?

If you could have any kind
of unconventional pet,
what would you choose?

What is the best reason
you can think of not to use
alcohol or drugs?

conversation starters for families

Bestow a "Fruit of the Spirit Award"
(Galatians 5:22-23) upon each family member.
From the following, affirm the quality
you observed recently.

☐ love ☐ joy ☐ peace

☐ patience ☐ goodness ☐ faithfulness

☐ gentleness ☐ kindness ☐ self-control

What dessert do you

think you could eat

for a lifetime?

In Acts 12 young Rhoda told the people in the house that Peter was knocking on the door, but they didn't believe her. Can you recall a time that you were telling the truth but someone didn't believe you?

If you could ask God

any question,

what would you ask?

question

**14**

conversation starters for families

Talk about a time when
it felt good to help someone.

If I could be any kind
of animal for a day,
I'd like to be a . . .

question

**16**

conversation starters for families

Which of the following would you like to have in your backyard?

- [ ] go-cart track
- [ ] swimming pool
- [ ] greenhouse
- [ ] miniature golf course
- [ ] tennis court
- [ ] clubhouse
- [ ] treehouse
- [ ] underground headquarters
- [ ] 20 pieces of playground equipment
- [ ] other _____

In the Chronicles of Narnia, four children walked through a wardrobe (clothes closet) and into the magical land of Narnia. If you had a magic door in the back of your closet that could take you to one special place anytime you want to go, where would it be?

What is something
that would be hard
for you to share?

As a surprise for your birthday party we've arranged for a famous person of your choice to attend.

Who will you choose?

I wish I had a

personal coach, tutor,

or mentor for . . .

What is one of the most uninteresting things you have to do on a regular basis?

Using the first letter of your first name, the family must come up with a positive word that begins with the same letter to describe you. For example: Talented Trevor or Generous Ginny.

What were the best and worst moments from this past week?

In what Olympic sports event would you like to win a gold medal?

Everyone has five minutes to scout the house for objects that positively describe members of the family, then use the object in a sentence to describe the person. For example: "I have a light-bulb for Cameron because he brings light into our house"; or "I have a paper clip for Mom because she holds our family together."

This week my internal weather
could be described as:

☐ partly cloudy ☐ partly sunny

☐ hot and dry ☐ unpredictable ☐ thunderstorms

☐ cold and rainy ☐ early fog, then clearing

☐ frost warning ☐ other _____

question
**27**

conversation starters for families

If at the end of every day you were granted an extra hour to do anything you wanted, how would you regularly spend that hour?

Tell family members about a compliment or affirmation that you've received recently from someone outside the family.

Who is someone in our extended family (grandparent, aunt, uncle, cousin, in-law) that you wish you could spend more time with?

Give each member of the family
an imaginary gift certificate
to a favorite store, for a favorite
or wished-for product, or
special event.

Who is someone in our extended family, neighborhood, school, church, or workplace for whom we could do something helpful? What could we do?

## About bullies

CHILDREN:

Who is the biggest bully at your school?

PARENTS:

Recall a bully at your school.

BOTH:

Why do you think some kids become mean?

**About trading places**

CHILDREN: I think the best part about

being a grown-up would be . . .

PARENTS: I think the best part about

being a kid again would be . . .

## The early years

PARENTS:

Recall and describe some special detail or feeling you remember about the day each child was born or came into the family.

CHILDREN:

What is your earliest childhood memory (one of the first that comes to mind)?

If you were President of the United States for a day, who is someone that you would honor with a special award?

What is your favorite
television commercial?

If you could change anything
about your appearance,
what would you change?

question

**38**

conversation starters for families

What is your favorite time of the day?

Favorite day of the week?

Favorite month of the year?

Recall a family outing or vacation that went badly but you're able to laugh about now.

Complete this sentence:
"I feel especially close
to you when . . ."

What was your best day
this past week?

question

42

conversation starters for families

What animal best illustrates
how you deal with conflict?

- [ ] lion—attack first
- [ ] turtle—turn inward and silent
- [ ] bird—fly away
- [ ] skunk—fight dirty
- [ ] snake—attack if provoked
- [ ] puppy—whimper and cry
- [ ] peacock—make a scene
- [ ] other_____

PARENTS:

A rule that I wish we had

in my family growing up is . . .

CHILDREN:

A rule in our family I wish

I could change is . . .

Talk about a time you were scared.

Conflict is pretty normal in all families. Forgiveness is a gift regularly offered in healthy families. Complete the following sentence: "(Name), I'm glad you're not still angry at me for . . ."

Recall a time when someone

(not a family member)

hurt your feelings.

Recall a time when you were nervous about having to do something in front of a lot of people (recitation, give a report or speech, sing, play an instrument, play a sport, etc.).

Recall a time that you were really embarrassed.

Complete this sentence:

"I wish I had the (courage, time,

or money) to try . . ."

Recently I didn't feel very

pleased with myself when I . . .

Each person comes up with a separate
answer for every family member:
"I know that something
that drives you nuts is . . ."

How much influence do you think your friends have on you?

If the Fruit of the Spirit (Galatians 5:22-23) grew on trees, which one would you most want to plant in our yard for yourself?

☐ love ☐ joy ☐ peace

☐ patience ☐ goodness

☐ faithfulness ☐ gentleness

☐ kindness ☐ self-control

What is something that you are worried about these days (or typically worry about)?

Tell about a time
you felt very sad.

Each person has a love language, a way in which they feel truly loved. What do you think is the love language of each person in our family?

- [ ] Physical touch (hugs, kisses, cuddling)
- [ ] Words of affirmation ("I love you," "I missed you today," "You look great")
- [ ] Acts of service (doing something special to help or surprise)
- [ ] Quality time (spending time together in a way that is meaningful for the other)
- [ ] Receiving gifts (tokens of love; items the person likes or enjoys)

One of the things that I like
most about our church
(or community) is . . .

Recall a family experience involving one of the following: fishing, hunting, biking, hiking, or camping.

The lion, beaver, otter, and golden retriever are animals used to describe four personality types. Which one do you think best describes you?

☐ I'm a lion: strong, confident, a leader; I like to make sure things get done.

☐ I'm a beaver: detail-oriented and organized. I follow instructions and am good with projects.

☐ I'm an otter: very outgoing, humorous, creative. I enjoy people.

☐ I'm a golden retriever: loyal, sensitive, caring.

Recall a family memory involving

one of the following:

☐ zoo  ☐ theme park

☐ sporting event  ☐ playground

☐ carnival  ☐ circus

Recall a funny family time

involving one of the following:

☐ fresh snow ☐ slick ice

☐ beach sand ☐ fall leaves

☐ gloppy mud

Describe two things
that happened today and
how you felt about
each of them.

Recall a family moment
at one of the following:

☐ ocean ☐ lake ☐ pond ☐ river

☐ creek ☐ mountain stream

☐ waterfall

question

**64**

conversation starters for families

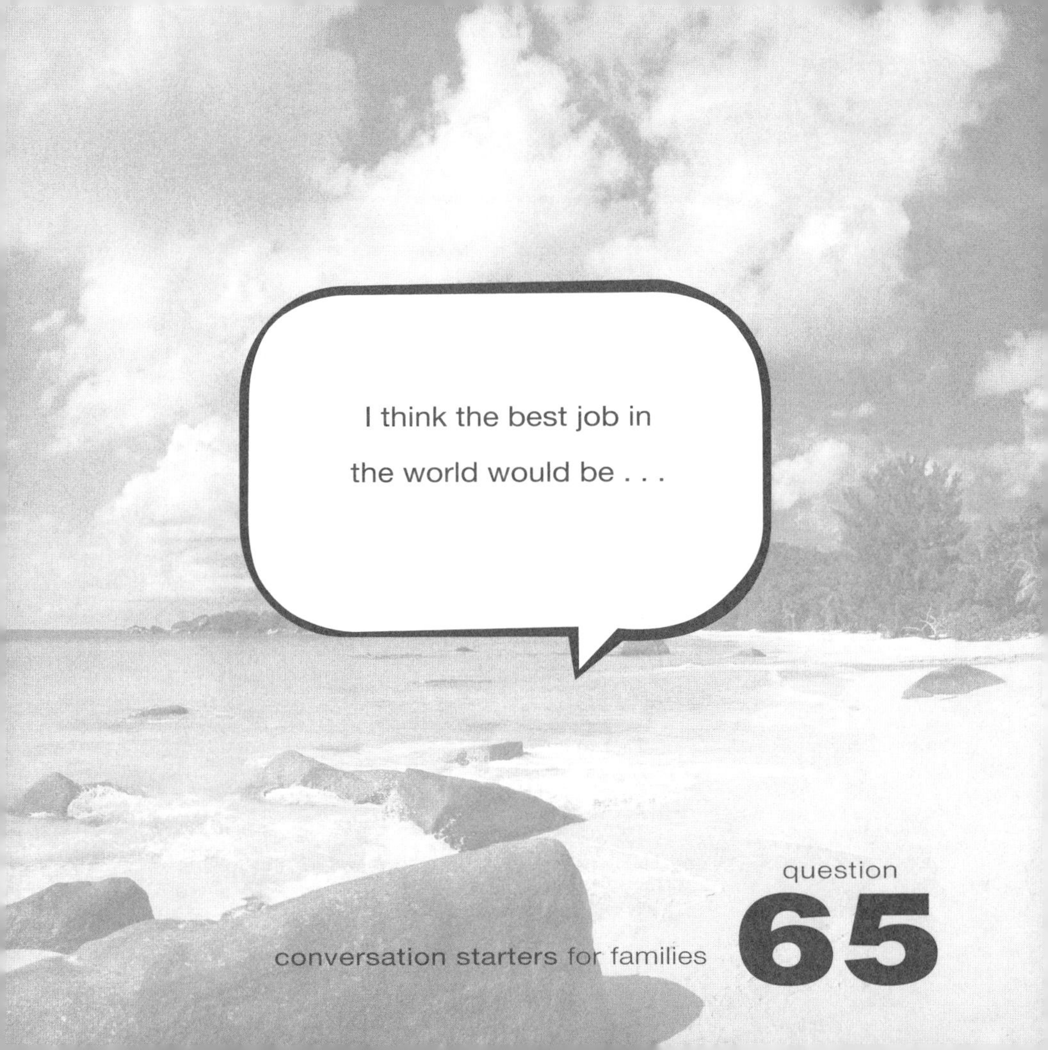

I think the best job in
the world would be . . .

question

**65**

CHILDREN:

What is your favorite toy?

What is your favorite candy?

PARENTS:

What were some of your favorite toys?

Some of your favorite candy?

You remind me of

Jesus the Healer

Jesus the Servant

Jesus the Preacher

Jesus the Storyteller

Jesus the Revolutionary

Our family has been invited to join the

Ringling Brothers, Barnum & Bailey Circus.

What role will you perform?

Which would you least like to do?

Recall a family experience

involving one of the following:

☐ a bike ride   ☐ a boat ride

☐ a plane ride   ☐ a train ride

☐ a carnival ride

When have you felt like an outsider—like you weren't part of the group?

One of television's most popular game shows was *Let's Make a Deal*, offering the risk of gain and loss. If Monty Hall, the host, were to say to you, "You can keep the $3,000 or trade it for what's behind the curtain," what would you do?

What is something in nature (plants, animals, fish, geography, weather, space, etc.) that truly fascinates you?

Of whom would you like to have an autographed photo?

Each person is to flip a coin and answer the appropriate question below.

HEADS: What was something encouraging or positive that happened today?

TAILS: What was something disappointing or difficult that happened today?

For this conversation starter,
each person will need a paper or
Styrofoam cup. Each person is to craft
(that is, draw, color, cut, tear, poke holes,
or attach objects to) his or her cup
in order to illustrate one of the following:

☐ How I feel today or this week

☐ My spiritual life right now

Pick one aroma that

makes you say "Aaahhhh."

☐ fresh brewed coffee ☐ fresh baked brownies

☐ new leather ☐ steaks broiling on a charcoal grill

☐ new car interior ☐ fresh baked bread

☐ honeysuckle in the breeze ☐ newly cut Christmas tree

Now come up with an additional

favorite scent on your own.

Complete this sentence: "I know you've heard me say it before, but I just want to tell you again: . . ." (Be original; say something other than "I love you.")

If our house were on fire and everyone (including pets) was safe outside and you could safely retrieve one personal item, what would it be?

Congratulations! You just foiled a robbery at one of your favorite stores. To say thanks, the manager has promised you a lifetime 50 percent discount. In what store will you be enjoying this savings?

Who is one of your favorite fictional characters? (This character may be from a book, short story, movie, video, television show, Saturday cartoon, comic book, or comic strip.)

What is one of your favorite sounds?

☐ a steady rain at night when I am in bed

☐ the bell signaling school is dismissed

☐ crickets chirping  ☐ my favorite music

☐ an ice cream truck chiming on the street

☐ ocean waves through the open window

☐ children laughing  ☐ coffee brewing in the morning

☐ a ringing phone, knowing it's for me

☐ other_____

Your family is burying a time capsule that will be opened one hundred years from now. What two items will each of you place in the capsule that illustrate something about your life right now?

If you could travel in the future to any time in your life to find out what happens or just to enjoy the moment, what period or moment in your life would you want to observe and why?

In the National Hockey League, the team that wins the championship receives a large trophy called the Stanley Cup. It is tradition that each member of the championship team enjoy personal possession of the Stanley Cup for a day. If you could take possession of anything in the world for one day, what would you choose?

If you were a country,

which would you be?

☐ Australia—mysterious and wild

    ☐ Israel—small but mighty

☐ Bahamas—warm and friendly

☐ United States—proud and ambitious

    ☐ Italy—inspiring

☐ Canada—big but gentle

☐ Japan—small but resourceful

    ☐ England—traditional

☐ Russia—dealing with changes and challenges

    ☐ France—elegant

The U.S. Postal Service has said that if you'll agree to be a mail carrier for the summer while some of their workers take vacation, they will provide you with the vehicle of your choice for your postal route. What's your choice of vehicle?

Which of the Seven Dwarfs are you today— Bashful, Dopey, Sleepy, Sneezy, Grumpy, Happy, or Doc?

CHILDREN:

What toy or activity most engages

your imagination or concentration?

PARENTS:

As a child or teen, what toy or activity most

engaged your imagination or concentration?

What pleasant activity most engages it now?

What product, service, place, or event are you so enthusiastic about that you'd make a good salesperson or spokesperson for it?

Something I'm looking forward to in the next few weeks or months is . . .

What do you think you would have said if Jesus had chosen you to be one of His twelve disciples? Recall a time that it felt good to be chosen by a person, group, team, or committee.

Recall a time when you were either not chosen for something or by someone. When was it? How did you feel?

In Luke 17 ten lepers were healed of their disease, but only one returned to thank Jesus. Think of something that each family member has done for you recently. Then express your thanks by saying, "I really appreciated it when you . . ." or "Thank you for . . ."

If you could ask Jesus to further explain something He said or did as recorded in the New Testament, what would you ask Him about?

Who is perhaps the best teacher you've ever had? Explain your choice.

question
95

CHILDREN:

What is something you remember

about a time you were very sick or injured?

PARENTS:

What is something you remember

about your children's illnesses or injuries?

Sometimes I wish I were more like (someone you know), because . . .

Pick any room in your home.
Using your imagination, how would
you like to remodel, redecorate,
and/or furnish the room?

Describe the

perfect Saturday.

conversation starters for families

Who is one of your favorite people in our church?

Before answering this last question you will want to give family members a chance to skim through the previous questions.

PARENTS:

Recall one of your child's responses that was especially interesting and meaningful to you. Tell everyone which one it was and why.

CHILDREN:

Recall one of the responses your parents gave to a question. Tell everyone which one it was and why.

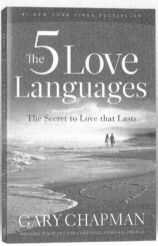
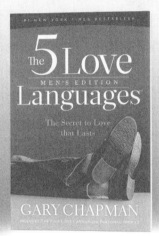

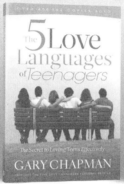

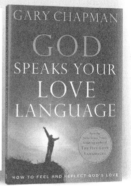

Learning your love language—and that of your spouse, teen, and child—might be the easiest and most important thing you ever learn. The assessments featured at www.5lovelanguages.com make it easy to discover your love language. Simply take one of our short profiles and find out how you and your loved one express and interpret love.

Right away, you can make a concerted effort to speak his or her primary language. It might not come naturally, but even the effort will be appreciated.

This dynamic site is also full of other helpful features—links to other resources, free stuff, upcoming events, podcasts, video, and more—all designed to encourage you and strengthen your relationships. We want to help you feel loved, and to effectively communicate love to others.

VISIT **5LOVELANGUAGES.COM**